921

Dove on the Roof

A collection of poems about peace

Also edited by Jennifer Curry

THE LAST RABBIT
Winner of the Earthworm Award

IN LOVE

Dove on the Roof

A collection of poems about peace

Selected by
JENNIFER CURRY

For Daphne Broad,
in peace and friendship

This anthology first published in Great Britain 1992
by Methuen Children's Books and Mammoth,
an imprint of Reed Consumer Books Limited
Michelin House, 81 Fulham Road, London SW3 6RB
and Auckland, Melbourne, Singapore and Toronto

Reprinted 1993

Copyright for this anthology © 1992
Methuen Children's Books Ltd

ISBN 0 7497 1056 X

A CIP catalogue record for this title
is available from the British Library

Typeset by Methuen Children's Books
Printed and bound in Great Britain
by Cox & Wyman Ltd, Reading, Berkshire

Contents

A Dove for Our Time   9

PART ONE   *What is Peace?* - Peace is a Promise

All in the Mind   Moira Andrew   13
The Dove   Rachel Wellman   14
Jimmy, Jimmy   Janis Priestley   15
Outbreak of Peace, haiku   Pie Corbett   16
Peace   Polly Smith   16
Peace in Our Time   Moira Andrew   17
Family Photo, '45   Susie Jenkin-Pearce   18
Haiku Friendship Poem   James Stevens   18
A Day Off   Ursula Laird   19
My Heart Beats   Ian Souter   20
Encounter   Robert Sparrow   22
Burn Your Lips   Elizabeth Wilkes   23
Deprivation   Emlyn Freeman   24
Destroyer Destroyed   Katie Redman   25
Why Must We Fight?   Paul   25
The Question   Sameera Khan   26

PART TWO   *War Games* - Teddy Bears, Dancing
Don't You Know There's a War On?   Brian Moses   29
Bang! Bang!   Anthony Dickinson   30
Desert Storm   Christopher Mann   31
Computer Game   Charles Thomson   32
Waterloo   Geoffrey Summerfield   34
After the Party   Robin Mellor   36
Newsflash   Adrian Henri   37

Attacking Missile Base Three   James Parsons   38
N.U.P. Report   Polly Sinclair   40
Russian Roulette   Adam Moon   41

PART THREE *After the Fighting* - Everyone Sang
Bombshell   Janis Priestley   45
Everyone Sang   Siegfried Sassoon   45
School Bus Journey - Malta, 1946   Anita Marie Sackett   46
The Soldiers Came   John Agard   47
 from *Harold*   James Waight   48
 Ash Talks to Bone   Joan Aiken   48
My Brother Coming Home   Meg Grant Turney   50
The Soldier's Home Coming   Rosie Filby   51
The Homecoming   Jean Kenward   52
A Lament   Wilfrid Wilson Gibson   53
Remembrance Day   Judith Nicholls   54

PART FOUR   *Is Peace Enough?* - Still No Potatoes
Post-war   Libby Houston   59
Arnhem   Christopher Mann   60
Light   Douglas Gibbons   62
Falklands Hero   Tom Masters   63
Tiananmen Square   Amy Shearing   64
Refugee   Jean Kenward   65
She a Brother, He a Hand   Li Chin   66
Sunrise in Kuwait   Liam Ring   66
The Red Cross   Theresa Heine   68
Epitaph for the Unknown Soldier   W.H. Auden   69
Christmas: 1924   Thomas Hardy   69
There Were No Potatoes   James Wolfe   70
The Search   Jamie Parkins   72

CONTENTS

Truces   Laura Blyth   73
If Peace Went on for Ever   William Payne   74
Peace   Ashley Bullard   75
Would You Swap?   Tony Roberts   76

PART FIVE   *Give Peace a Chance* - Silver Dream
I Dream of a Time   John Foster   79
Not a Piece of Cake   Lola Gamester   79
Silver Dream   Tony Roberts   80
Caged Bird   Trevor Harvey   82
Christopher's Song   Theresa Heine   83
Kid Stuff   Frank Horne   84
The Conclusion   Ian Souter   85
The Power of Love   Vernon Scannell   86
What's the Truth?   John Kitching   87
Why We Must Be Heroes   C. Livesey   88
Falklands Duty   Laurelle Rond   88
Throw It Away   Jonathan Hart   90
Bridge in the Sky   Theresa Heine   91
For the Christening of Princess Elizabeth
   William Shakespeare   92
Peace in a Bottle   Brian Moses   93
A Patch of Peace   Jane Whittle   94
Keeping the Peace   Celia Warren   95
On the Seventh Day   Ian Whybrow   96
To Every Thing   Ecclesiastes   98

Index of Poets   101
Index of First Lines   104
Acknowledgements   107

A Dove for Our Time

Peace and war are so mixed up together that it is almost impossible to separate them. They are like two sides of one coin, two halves of one whole.

When I was growing up during the war we thought about peace all the time. We were always talking about it, trying to imagine it, longing for it to come. We even dreamed about it. But we hardly ever called it by its name. For us, peace was 'before the war' or 'after the war'. The war was 'now'.

The same thing happened when I began to collect these poems. Every single one has something to say about peace, yet the word 'war' echoes from page after page.

Peace can only become a separate thing, instead of the other side of war, when we have at last managed to stop the fighting and killing that is always going on somewhere in the world. Then war will become just a memory and peace will be 'now'. We might even be able to throw away all the 'killing machines' and forget whatever we used to do with them.

Many children helped me to create this book by writing me poems to tell me what THEY thought about peace. I would like to thank them all, particularly the pupils of:

Debenham High School,
Halesworth Middle School,
Worlingham Church of England Primary School and
James Allen's Girls' School

who worked so hard, so willingly and so well.

I hope *Dove on the Roof* shows that the idea of a world at peace is not just an unrealistic dream. These poems are not sentimental. They are positive, forceful, even aggressive, about our need to strive for peace, and to hold on to it. The dove's wings are soft and feathered, but they are also strong. And he has powerful claws that reach out, and then *grip*.

JENNIFER CURRY

PART ONE

What is peace?
Peace is a Promise

All in the Mind

Peace is a bird,
white-feathered
as a winter tree
frothed in snow.

It is silence
leaking from cupped
hands like ice-cold
mountain water.

Peace is a petal
on the summer wind,
fine-spun as a
dragonfly's wing.

It is a promise
straddling the skies
like a rainbow
after the storm.

MOIRA ANDREW

The Dove

I am peace
I am a dove
I fly across the world
I try to land
In every country

But in some lands
They won't let me alight
They fire at me
And try to shoot me down
But I'll return and
I will try again

Perhaps tomorrow
They will let me land
But till tomorrow
I'll fly on my way
Maybe tomorrow
They will let me stay

RACHEL WELLMAN (12)

Jimmy, Jimmy

Jimmy, Jimmy?
Yes, young Fred.
Jimmy, Jimmy,
Have you heard the news?
No, young Fred.
They said that War is dead.

Jimmy, Jimmy?
Yes, young Fred.
Jimmy, Jimmy,
I've looked everywhere.
For what, young Fred?
They said that peace has come.

Jimmy, Jimmy.
Yes, young Fred.
Jimmy, Jimmy,
Will she be beautiful?
Who, young Fred?
Why, peace of course.

Oh, yes, young Fred.
She's beautiful all right.
Like a tumbling cascade
That's turned into a stream.
That's peace, young Fred.
Crystal clear and flowing everywhere.

Jimmy, Jimmy.
Yes, young Fred.
Will I know her when we meet?
Oh, yes, young Fred.
But whether you can keep her,
That, young Fred, is the problem.

JANIS PRIESTLEY

Outbreak of Peace, haiku

My mum declares peace.
She hands out bouquets of smiles.
Laughter like church bells.

PIE CORBETT

Peace

Flower
Power

POLLY SMITH (14)

Peace in Our Time

PEACE!
PEACE IN OUR TIME scream
the yellowing headlines.
A fuzzy photograph, an
old man in a Homburg hat
waves a piece of paper.

PEACE!
'Give me a bit of peace,'
yells my mother. We rattle
up and downstairs paying
not the slightest bit of
attention. Mother sighs.

PEACE!
The bells ring out. A new
era is ushered in. Children
of the war, knowing only
blackout and rations learn
the new taste of bananas.

PEACE!
'Grant me peace,' whispers
my mother as she lies dying.
Pain maps its contour lines
across her face. Her peace
is forever, ours touch and go.

MOIRA ANDREW

Family Photo, '45

Peace, for me, is a black and white photo,
Chubby little girl in a paper crown.
Frowning at the sun, she stands on a chair,
In a street that is full of chairs, and of children,
Food on the tables, bakelite beakers
With red and gleaming victory 'V's.
And she is embraced, safely secure,
Within her brother's broken arm.

SUSIE JENKIN-PEARCE

Haiku Friendship Poem

Two boys by firelight,
One black face the other white,
Friends in the cold night.

JAMES STEVENS (11)

18

A Day Off

I don't want
anything offensive
bothering me today
I have proclaimed
to my heart
that this will be
a clear clean
summer's day
no messing about
with dustbins
and other people's tragedies
no giving or taking
good advice
no guilt feelings about the past
just a sitting in the garden
watching-the-bees-work
sort of day.

URSULA LAIRD

My Heart Beats

My spirits tighten
when the television protests:

seas under threat,
oil pollution,
nuclear power.

When the radio complains of:

mountains of rubbish,
wastage of energy,
global warming.

When the newspapers cry:

acid rain,
holes in the ozone layer,
destroying the rain forests.

My spirits tighten.

But my heart beats
when I think of:

nothing moving,
only sunshine colouring in
as it spills itself across
a freshly made morning.

When I imagine:

snowflakes furtively
dusting themselves
in their talcum powder cleanliness
across an unsuspecting countryside.

When I listen:

to the night's silence
wrapping itself gently around me,
to await the creation
of a new born day.

My heart beats.

IAN SOUTER

Encounter

I found this small white church in Brittany
The door propped open with a stone.
I wondered why but then went in
And in the cool and white-washed silence sat alone.
Between rough benches of old unpainted wood
In quiet I sat, not offering prayer or praise,
But thought of people long since gone
Who had knelt here in far-off days.
I felt their presence in the silence
But lost in thought was taken by surprise
By steel-blue flash of sudden wings,
A swallow speeding past my eyes.

I had such feelings of contentment,
I could have told myself it was absurd
To sit down in an ancient church
And glad to share that moment with a bird.

ROBERT SPARROW

Burn Your Lips

Burn your lips with scalding coffee;
Slam the door;
Yell goodbye,
Impatient to be gone,
Yet not eager.
Screech to a stop
At the red light;
Wait forty minutes
In the traffic jam.
Frown,
Curse the other drivers,
Who are cursing you.
Finally make it.
Hand your work on to the next person,
Who hands it on
Until
It's lost.
Home at last!
Have a drink;
Forget it all;
Just survive until
Tomorrow is today.
Be thankful;
Freedom allows your opinions
To be spoken
And lost in the trickle
Of satirical laughter.
Be thankful;

Have what you will;
Don't go without.
Give to others
That they may be as fortunate
And live
In a land at peace.

ELIZABETH WILKES (14)

Deprivation

What!
No football league?
No Super Blues?
No Canaries?
Did they grow lettuce at the Layer?
Did they raise rhubarb at Roots Hall?
Did they breed pigs at Portman Road?
What would I have done
On Saturday afternoons?
How filled the evenings
Without 'Sun Sport'?
How would I have lived
Without my football?
I'm glad I'm not
A war time boy.

EMLYN FREEMAN (14)

Destroyer Destroyed

In the ocean a ship lies
Amongst the coral and weeds.
Its guns are silent.
Round a port hole lurks a shark;
In the cabins, fish swim between the bunks;
They own the ship.
They hatch their young
In machines
That long ago took life.
Their home
Was once a Destroyer.
Shark and fish
Live together in peace.

KATIE REDMAN (13)

Why Must We Fight?

Why must we have war?
Why must we fight?
Why can't we be friends?
Why can't things be right?

PAUL (9)

25

The Question

What do you
call war? Hate.
What do you
call murder?
Hate.
What
do you
call dis-
crim-
ination?
Hate.
What do
you call
fear?
Hate.
What do
you call
peace?

LOVE. LO-
VE. LOVE. L-
OVE. LOVE. LOVE.
LOVE. LOVE. L-
OVE. LOVE.
LOVE.

SAMEERA KHAN (13)

26

PART TWO

War games
Teddy Bears, Dancing

Don't You Know There's a War On?

My mother didn't know there was a war on!
She hung out her washing on the line
as I crouched among the cabbages
and gave covering fire.

My father didn't know there was a war on!
He called out 'Hello,' as he came back from work
and I broke cover, shouted back,
ignoring the cracking of bullets.

The dog didn't know there was a war on!
He carried on sniffing in No Man's Land
then cocked a leg on the sign I'd painted
to warn of the danger from mines.

The neighbours didn't know there was a war on!
They hung over our fence and complained
that one of my missiles went A.W.O.L.
and drove its way through the dahlias.

After that I jacked in the war,
ran up a white flag and agreed to end
hostilities for the day. I pulled out my troops
from the flower beds, brought back the dead
to life, and then boxed them all and went indoors.

There wasn't much for tea and when
I complained Mum snapped, 'I thought you said
there's a war on, and how am I supposed
to bring supplies through a battle zone?'

Later I watched 'The News' on TV.
It seemed there was a war on everywhere.
Perhaps I'll declare an outbreak of peace tomorrow!

BRIAN MOSES

Bang! Bang!

What do they know of war,
Little kids,
Who play with guns
And kill their friends
One by one?
How they long
To fight for Queen and Country!
But,
They would come back
Crying,
With scarlet memories.

ANTHONY DICKINSON (14)

Desert Storm

Cable News Network bring you live and exclusive coverage,
with the first film of the A-10 tank-busters in action;
screaming in across the desert to break up the enemy formations;
Notice the precision bombing of the laser-guided smart weapons,
maximum force with minimum off-target damage:

Sega and Nintendo bring you the video game of the age;
with the first simulation of the A-10 tank-busters in action;
screaming in across the screen to break up the enemy formations;
Notice the precision graphics of the microchip explosions,
maximum excitement at minimum expense:

Saddam Hussein brings you the death of your village,
with the first attacking wave of the world's reaction;
screaming in across the desert to break apart your nation;
Notice the precision demolition of your schools and houses,
maximum suffering with minimum excuse.

CHRISTOPHER MANN

Computer Game

WHAM! WHAM! Zappa zappa!
Zappa zappa zoom!
There's a manic computer game
up in my room.

As soon as I switch off
the lamp every night
enemy space ships
appear on the right:

ZOOP-ZOOP! ZOOP-ZOOP!
Beep-beep-beep.
The noises it makes
stop me going to sleep.

Now as the main
invasion fleet nears
I snug in my pillow
with plugs in my ears.

ZAPOW! ZAP! ZAP-ZAP!
ZAP! POW-POW!
As you may have guessed,
I'm wideawake now.

Zip-zip! Zeep-zeep!
Zip! BAM-BAM!
The rockets rush,
the lasers slam,

the deck guns splat,
the ray guns blast,
each invader explodes
as it rushes past.

Bip-bip, bip-bip,
zeep-zeep ZAM!
Just one to go – look out!
BAM! BAM!

My ship is moving
in the deep.
Beep-beep, beep-beep,
beep beep beep.

The sky is black,
my ship is steady;
I open my eyes –
It's morning already!

CHARLES THOMSON

Waterloo

Napoleon, the roly-poly 'un,
And Skellington, the bony 'un,
Made a great hullabaloo
At the Battle of Waterloo.

They stared at each other
And they shouted rude names.
'I'll go and tell my mother
If you try your old games.'

Bony fired his water-pistol
And stuck out his tongue.
Welly said, 'Watch it! My fist'll
Bop your nose before long.'

They threw bits of bricks.
They threw sticks and stones.
Bony said, 'Try any tricks,
And I'll break all your bones.'

Then Welly cried, 'Pax!
There's something in my eye.'
Bony stopped in his tracks.
'Let me help. I can try.'

34

So they sat down together
And they fixed Welly's eye.
He said, 'I don't know whether
To laugh or cry.'

Then they turned out their pockets –
It was time for a break.
Welly found some biscuits
To go with Bony's bit of cake.

'What shall we do now?'
Said Welly, then frowned.
'Oh, I'm in for a row,
I forgot my paper round!'

GEOFFREY SUMMERFIELD

After the Party

After the party
crackers lie broken on the floor,
party hats have been discarded
and streamers hang over the door.

My ears are singing
with the quiet of the room
where, just a little while ago,
voices yelled and records boomed.

Mum says it looks
as if a bomb has hit the place,
and would I, before we clean up,
wipe the jelly from my face?

Grandad sometimes tells me
about the bombs that fell in the war,
but Grandma always stops him
before he can tell me more.

I think the peace
that followed an air raid on the town
must have been like after the party,
with dusty silence all around.

ROBIN MELLOR

Newsflash

Reports are just coming in that . . .

THE TOYS HAVE TAKEN OVER TOYTOWN!
After fierce fighting in the hills above Nutwood
The Famous Five have succeeded in capturing the Chalet School
and have linked up with forces
led by Algy the Pug and Rupert Bear.
Tintin and Captain Haddock,
after making the perilous approach by sea,
have taken the harbour without a struggle.

Noddy and Big Ears
lead the triumphal motorcade down the High Street
followed by the tramp tramp tramp of feet
of the Mister Men. Paddington Bear
and The Railway Children
ride Thomas the Tank Engine.

Mr Quelch and Ernest the Policeman
have fled into exile.
Postman Pat has taken over the Radio Station,
broadcasts an appeal for calm to the nation,
proclaims a new democratic regime,
free sweets for all,
the abolition of bedtime.

As dusk falls on riot-torn Toytown
the air is filled with laughter,
the munching of chocolate
and the soft sound of teddy bears,
dancing.

ADRIAN HENRI

Attacking Missile Base Three

I ran across the long playground.
I jumped behind some stumpy logs.
ZAP! ZAP!
My lazer-blaster fired.
I ran past the crystallized being.
'Missile Bases One and Two destroyed,' my CB crackled.
Twzap! ZAP!
I jumped over the ruins of Missile Base Two.
A loud explosion,
A big bang,
A shower of sparks.
I threw myself down.
BANG!!!
POW!
PLANG!
KOWPANG!
BANG!!
I was engulfed in flames.

I got up,
Brushed the bits of iron off myself,
'Mission completed,' I said.
Life-support-suit burnt,
I walked through the smoke,
Then had a rest.
Dead silence.
Missile Base Three blasterized.
'Three down and one to go,' cackled Ben on the radio,
ZAP!
Another bogeyman I thought.

> ZAP!
> ZAP!
> POW!
> ZAP!
> POW!
> POW!
> ZAP!
> ARRRGGHH!!
> Silence.
> From the flames I approached it . . .
> I threw down the pin,
> I threw the rugger ball,
> ORRING! the bell went.
> I went into the missile base
> ULTIMATE.

JAMES PARSONS (9)

N.U.P. Report

The National Union
of Peacemakers
held
their annual conference
at Peacehaven.

Delegates arrived
from Concord, Massachusetts,
but
none was invited
from Wargrave or Warminster.

During the teabreak
they played
'Kiss
In The Ring'.
War Games were vetoed.

A peaceful day
was enjoyed by
all,
and nobody gave anybody
a peace of their mind.

POLLY SINCLAIR

Russian Roulette

They sat opposite;
A table in between.
Illuminated, the gun lay cold.
The lean grey Eagle raised
The weapon to its forehead.
It pulled the trigger – nothing.
It smiled.

The Bear did the same,
A click came forth,
It grinned.

But,
What neither of them realized was,
That neither of them could win

Because,
A Dove had plucked the
Bullet from the chamber.

They sat at that table for
Infinity.

ADAM MOON (16)

PART THREE

After the fighting Everyone Sang

Bombshell

Last night
Bombs fell,
Tonight
Like a bombshell
Fell peace.

JANIS PRIESTLEY

Everyone Sang

Everyone suddenly burst out singing;
And I was filled with such delight
As prisoned birds must find in freedom
Winging wildly across the white
Orchards and dark-green fields; on; on; and out of sight.

Everyone's voice was suddenly lifted,
And beauty came like the setting sun.
My heart was shaken with tears; and horror
Drifted away . . . O but every one
Was a bird; and the song was wordless; the singing will
  never be done.

SIEGFRIED SASSOON

School Bus Journey – Malta, 1946

They were part of the landscape,
Twisted heaps of metal
In the parched fields
By the roadside.
Prickly pear cactus and white stone walls
Framed them.
They flashed by the bus windows.
'Dakotas,' they were explained.
'Crashed in the war.'

Sitting on the bus
She worried about division
And multiplication,
And learning 'The Lord's Prayer',
Yet was curious about the planes,
Wrecks, gutted and pillaged.
Mementoes of a war
She knew nothing about,
Over, a year before.

ANITA MARIE SACKETT

The Soldiers Came

The soldiers came
and dropped their bombs.
The soldiers didn't take long
to bring the forest down.

With the forest gone
the birds are gone.
With the birds gone
who will sing their song?

But the soldiers forgot
to take the forest
out of the people's hearts.
The soldiers forgot
to take the birds
out of the people's dreams.
And in the people's dreams
the birds still sing their song.

Now the children
are planting seedlings
to help the forest grow again.
They eat a simple meal of soft rice
wrapped in banana leaf.
And the land welcomes their smiling
like a shower of rain.

JOHN AGARD

from *Harold*

Britons and Romans, Saxons and then Danes,
So many conquerors have taken it,
I somdel wonder any land is left.
Yet oak-trees grow, and daisies star the grass,
And blissful birds sing blithely as of yore;
Sheep bleateth, and the mild-eyed cattle chaw
Their peaceful cud. Men waggon up the hay
And ear the soil and breed the olden way
As if the conquerors had never passed.

JAMES WAIGHT

Ash Talks to Bone

The ghost of a cuckoo
in a skeleton tree
called a promise
to the ghost of me –

a ghostly cuckoo
in a skeleton larch
in doubtful april
or spectral march

take heart, take heart
called the ghostly bird
(or this is what
I thought I heard)

you and I
are ash and bone
you and I
are dead and gone

but seeds are waiting
under all
trees will grow again
strong and tall

deep in the future
centuries past
nuclear night
will end at last

dawn will break
and life rejoice
in unknown words
and a foreign voice

take heart, take heart
called the ghostly bird
(or this is what
I thought I heard)

JOAN AIKEN

My Brother Coming Home

'Here,' said Mam. 'Hold one end of this old sheet
and I'll take the other.' So we stood
at opposite sides of the room and she snipped
with the steel scissors a strip a metre wide.

'Here,' said Mam. 'Use the marker pen,'
and I spread the strip flat in the yard
and wrote carefully all along
in red capitals, 'Welcome home, David.'

I tied strings to each end and Jo went upstairs
in Mam and Dad's room, and I in Aunt Edie's house
across the street, and we slung the banner
between the grey stone terraces, waiting for my brother.

Aunt Edie vacuumed and Nan polished,
Dad bought in beer and Coke and crisps,
Jo made sausage rolls, I stuck things on cocktail sticks.
Mam baked a chocolate celebration cake.

Then at last it was evening and my brother was
coming home safe, strolling up the street,
dark hair cropped short, and shoulders square,
swinging his bag, a great grin on his suntanned face,

dropping his bag, throwing his arms open to hug.

MEG GRANT TURNEY

The Soldier's Home Coming

My father.
Who is this man?
I don't remember a father
Who would take me to the park
And buy me sweets.
I was jealous of my friend.
She had a father.
And he was kind.

But I do vaguely remember a man
Who smoked a pipe
And never wore socks.
Perhaps this was my father.

He'll be home soon.
My mother's excited.
But I can't understand why.

This man with the stubbly beard . . .
What will he be like now?
Will he still smell of black coffee?
My mother used to make him
Clean his boots in front of the fire.

Tonight . . .
This man will come home
And be part of us again.

ROSIE FILBY (13)

The Homecoming

It's good, coming home,
    but I miss the chaps in the tank corps –
the men that slept and ate with me
    day by day,
the jokes and companionship
    in dirt and danger,
and opening letters that found us
    so far away.

It's good to be home:
    the kids have grown beyond measure.
They seem to think
    I'm a bit of a stranger here.
It'll take time, they say,
    for things to settle . . .
some weeks, or months perhaps.
    Even a year.

I was glad to get home.
    The pub is still on the corner
but the man who sits in my chair
    has a different face,
and the children I knew
    have turned into teenagers;
and the house that I held in my heart
    is a different place.

JEAN KENWARD

A Lament

We who are left, how shall we look again
Happily on the sun, or feel the rain,
Without remembering how they who went
Ungrudgingly, and spent
Their all for us, loved, too, the sun and rain?

A bird among the rain-wet lilac sings –
But we, how shall we turn to little things
And listen to the birds and winds and streams
Made holy by their dreams,
Nor feel the heart-break in the heart of things?

WILFRID WILSON GIBSON

Remembrance Day – 11th November

Poppies? Oh, miss,
can I take round the tray?
It's only history next.
We're into '45 –
I KNOW who won the war,
no need to stay.

Old man wears his flower
with pride, his numbers dying now –
but that's no news.

Why buy? –
because I'm asked
because a flower looks good
to match my mate
not to seem too mean –
(what's tenpence anyway
to those of us who grew
with oranges, December lettuce
and square fish?)
Yes, I'll wear it –
for a while.
Until it's lost
or maybe picked apart
during some boring television news
and then, some idle moment,
tossed.

Poppies? Who cares
as long as there's
some corner of a foreign field
to bring me pineapple, papaya
and my two weeks' patch of sun? –
But I'll still have one
if you really want.
It isn't quite my scene but then
at least the colour's fun.

*Old man stumbles
through November mud,
still keeps his silence
at the eleventh hour.*

JUDITH NICHOLLS

PART FOUR

Is Peace Enough?
Still No Potatoes

Post-war

In 1943
my father
dropped bombs on the continent

I remember
my mother
talking about bananas
in 1944

when it rained,
creeping alone to the windowsill,
I stared up the hill,
watching, watching,
watching without a blink
for the Mighty Bananas
to stride through the blitz

they came in paper bags
in neighbours' hands
when they came
and took their time
over the coming

and still I don't know
where my father
flying home
took a wrong turning

LIBBY HOUSTON

Arnhem

23.9.84
We didn't want to come here, but they made us:
On a hot Sunday when the beach is better
than an old graveyard under the dark and gloomy trees.
But Dad said: 'We're going,' and that was that.

So many stones, sticking out of the neat grass,
carved with names, dates, ages:
And all kinds of people: Poles, Scots, English, German . . .
Lying asleep in Holland, in the neat grass.

People pushed and shoved in the museum –
I could hardly see the video, or the uniforms and guns,
and the rows of shiny medals;
The tanks and guns were magic, but now it's time to go.

23.9.44
We didn't want to come here, but they made us:
On a hot Saturday when anywhere is better
than a muddy shellhole under the dark and gloomy trees.
But the General said:'We're going,' and that was that.

So many bodies, slumped in the trampled grass,
Labelled with names, dates, ages:
All kinds of people: Poles, Scots, English, German . . .
Lying dead in Holland, in the trampled grass.

Soldiers pushed and shoved in the ruined hotel –
I could hardly see the window for the uniforms and guns,
and the rows of medal ribbons;
The tanks and guns were magic, but now it's time to go.

CHRISTOPHER MANN

Light

His hands rummaged
Through the wooden chest.
A belt, a bag, a gas globe –
Then a tin hat was revealed,
Its metal dusty and old.
It fitted over his eyebrows;
The straps hung loose beneath his chin.
It had been his grandfather's hat.
His fingers felt the dented shell.
'It's broken, Dad. What happened?'

His dad turned;
Memories flooded like the mustard gas
That had threatened his father.
He told of the bomb shelter,
How concrete and mud had swept in,
How he, as a child,
Wearing his father's helmet
From that other war,
Had dived under a bed.

'But no one got hurt, Dad,
Not really hurt?'
He understood nothing;
His innocence knew no darkness,
Just the light of freedom.
But, without the dark
Those other men had known,
There could be no light
For the boy.

DOUGLAS GIBBONS (15)

Falklands Hero

I saw a man on telly,
It was his wedding day.
His bride looked proud and cheerful,
Throwing her bouquet.
And he seemed really happy
As he gripped her hand so tight.
They stood there smiling bravely –
But something wasn't right.

The man's a Falklands hero,
The news presenter said.
He went through flames and torment
With burning hands and head.
His friends were trapped and dying,
He tried to drag them free.
His face was burnt to cinders.
They thought he'd never see.

But now he has a new face.
The doctors made him one
With grafted skin and tissue
And neatly-mended bone.
He looks a little different,
But he's lucky to be here –
A happy man, a bridegroom,
With nothing more to fear.

I saw a man on telly,
His face was not quite right,
The mouth so strangely twisted,
The skin so shiny bright.
They all say that he's lucky –
Does he ask them why?
Dare he look in the mirror?
And does it make him cry?

TOM MASTERS

Tiananmen Square

Red rose-buds stood there proud and tall,
fighting against the concrete world.
They did not fight with thorns
but with the beauty of their youth.
They stood there in a small, compacted square,
surrounded by concrete hate.
But then a man passed by and saw the buds of life
and with his scissors he ignorantly cut
the adolescent deep red buds.
And on the Square, once innocent,
a carpet of bloody petals lay.
A cruel smile swept over that man's face.
But he had not won.
For next year, where buds of red once stood,
I found the yellow rose,
the rose of peace.

AMY SHEARING (12)

Refugee

This was my home.
I lived here all my life,
till secretly they came
and burned it down . . .
Now, there is nothing left:
only a name
on the charred wood
that none will read
or know.
I watched the flames,
and saw the whole house
go.

So I have nowhere special
of my own
to stay – nowhere to sleep
or be alone.
The days are drenched in sadness,
and no word
speaks to a boy who –
like a wounded bird –
limps to and fro
trailing a broken wing,
not finding food, love, water –
anything.

JEAN KENWARD

65

She a Brother, He a Hand

When at last the gun shots cease
And deathly silence reigns
Some people thank God for their lives
Some count ill-gotten gains.
Friend and foe embrace and vow
Between them peace will last somehow.

For what were they fighting? A piece of land.
For this she lost a brother, he a hand.

LI CHIN (11)

Sunrise in Kuwait

Bright,
Majestic,
The sun rises,
Revealing a land
Of unsuspecting,
Over confident people.
If you said,
'Danger,'
They would laugh.
'Look at our beaches,
Our lustrous seas.'

66

Now,
Enveloped in red
Sheet-like clouds,
The sun descends,
Leaving a land
Of unsuspecting,
Over confident people.

Dull,
Dejected,
The sun struggles up,
Shedding an oily light
Over a land
Of rejected people.
Look at them with
Their mine ridden shore
And ebony sea.
Now,
Enveloped in a curtain of black lace,
Our sun dies,
Abandoning a land
Of rejected,
Uncared for people.

LIAM RING (12)

The Red Cross

April 5th 1990
Dear Frau Schmidt,
              We are pleased to inform you
that we have been able to trace your son Hannes,
reported missing in Dresden during an air-raid
on June 9th 1944. He is alive and well and living
in Munich.
              We enclose his photo and address.
                   We wish you joy in your reunion.
                        With best wishes

THERESA HEINE

Epitaph for the Unknown Soldier

To save your world, you asked this man to die:
Would this man, could he see you now, ask why?

W. H. AUDEN

Christmas: 1924

'Peace upon earth!' was said. We sing it,
And pay a million priests to bring it.
After two thousand years of mass
We've got as far as poison gas.

THOMAS HARDY

There Were No Potatoes

There were no potatoes.
The woman in the middle of the queue,
Stamped her feet,
To keep out the chill.
The frost crunched in the square,
Under the heavy boots of the soldiers.
A man walked into the church,
The vaulted ceiling high above,
He thought of days gone by,
The clear air carried the bite of winter,
A child threw a snowball,
Into the air,
He wandered through the city streets.
A scrawny cat whined.
He made his way into the square.
The woman in the queue,
Envied his innocence.
He stopped to pull the arm of a soldier.
The soldier shrugged him off with a smile.
The child of a poor world,
Surrounded by riches.

The golden domes stood in the sky,
A symbol of equality and death,
They glittered in the cold light.
Inside men worked,
To make the world a better place,
A country for the children.
Great plans,
Of reform and revolution,
Loosening bonds,
Strengthening ties.
Improving the houses,
Stopping the killing in the streets,
Giving the right to hear,
And to be heard,
The grand design,
A country fit for heroes,
A jewel in the world of men.
One man,
Risking his life for the people,
Giving them another chance,
A better way,
And there were still no potatoes.

JAMES WOLFE (13)

The Search

With bright blonde hair
And tiny frame,
She runs through
English countryside,
Trying to escape
Mummy's angry cries,
Under clear skies,
Past glistening streams,
Over dewed grass,
Searching for peace.
How can her innocence
Find the goal
When she can not know
What to look for?

With dirty hair
And tiny frame,
She runs around
The bleak, wet hills.
She is trying
To escape from
Those war-torn skies
And war-torn cries.
This Kurdish child may reach
Her goal of peace
For, taught by war,
She knows
What to look for.

JAMIE PARKINS (15)

Truces

One Saturday morning
When I was having my breakfast
Carl my brother
Started to kick me
Under the breakfast table
For no reason!
So I said, 'Stop it.'
'No!' said Carl.
And then we started arguing
And we never stopped since.
Then, when Tuesday came
(Which was my birthday)
My brother and I made up.

But on Wednesday
Carl kicked me
Under the breakfast table.

LAURA BLYTH (9)

If Peace Went on for Ever

If peace went on for ever it would be dull and boring,
but some people seem to like sleeping and snoring.

You see, it might be the wrong thing to do
but I really ENJOY a fight or two.

Wars may be horrible and nasty
and even guns are ghastly.

Yes, we all hate war, war, war,
but maybe . . . we need . . . just ONE more?

WILLIAM PAYNE (9)

Peace

An oil rig leaked a week ago
there was a bomb attack
two days ago
but now there's peace.

The attacking country thought
that the people forgot
the bombing plot.
Probably not!

ASHLEY BULLARD (9)

Would You Swap?

From our Laboratory comes –
A New Improved
Formula for peace.
Using Special rays,
It actually
Cleans whiter than white,
Removing dirt,
Stubborn grease
And odours.
This New triple-action
Peace-product
Is concentrated
And, if placed
On the world,
(It starts working
Straight away –
From the centre of the wash)
Will rid the earth
Of its blemishes,
Leaving perfection.
Just open the
Easy-pour,
Lead-lined lid,
To use –
New,
Improved,
Radiation.™

TONY ROBERTS (15)

PART FIVE

Give peace a chance
Silver Dream

I Dream of a Time

I dream of a time

When the only blades are blades of corn
When the only barrels are barrels of wine
When the only tanks are full of water
When the only chains are chains of hands

I hope for a time . . .

JOHN FOSTER

Not a Piece of Cake

This is a poem about peace,
It's hard to make it work.
Peace is like my poem.
It's not a piece of cake.

LOLA GAMESTER (13)

Silver Dream

His was
A silver dream of peace,
Equality for men,
No black or white,
Just silver;
No rioting again.

One voice
Shouted out from the mumble,
One voice
To set wrongs right;
One voice
With a million echoes,
The voice of
Martin Luther King.

One leaden mind,
One leaden fist,
One leaden trigger pulled,
One leaden bullet
Glinting death
Slashed against the dreamer.

The silver melted
To a poppy red
Then hardened to black mourning,
Tarnished silver
Ridden with grief,
With protests
And with rioting.

Inspired by the dream,
New silver came,
New wisdom and rejoicing;
The silver dreamer may have died
But the dream lives on
Still shining.

TONY ROBERTS (13)

Caged Bird

skywards,
the song
e s c a p e s –

$$g$$
$$n$$
$$i$$
$$o \qquad t$$
$$l \qquad a$$
$$f$$

upward –
m e l t i n g
outward –
its soul
forever
free,
though
the world
may hold it
prisoner

TREVOR HARVEY

Christopher's Song

It was cold and foggy,
And the waiting was long
At the crossing point,
And the humming grew
To a swell of noise
When the barricade lifted,
And cheers hit the sky
As West met East
In a blaze of cameras
And roses and wine
And hugging and kissing,
And carrying shoulder high
Through the streets of Berlin.
And I was there
On the Wall with them,
And we all held hands
And danced and cheered,
November the 9th!
That night of joy, of tears.

THERESA HEINE

NOTE: *In 1961 a huge fortified wall was built across Berlin to divide Eastern Germany, ruled by the Russians, from Western Germany, which was occupied by the Western Allies. In 1989, as a sign of peace, the Wall was pulled down and Germany was united again.*

Christopher was taken by his parents to watch the Wall begin to fall and join in the celebrations.

Kid Stuff

The wise guys
tell me
that Christmas
is kid stuff . . .
Maybe they've got
something there –
Two thousand years ago
three wise guys
chased a star
across a continent
to bring
frankincense and myrrh
to a Kid
born in a manger
with an idea in his head . . .

And as the bombs
crash
all over the world today
the real wise guys know
that we've all got to go
chasing stars
again
in the hope
that we can get back
some of that
kid stuff
born two thousand years ago.

FRANK HORNE

The Conclusion

I have arrived at a conclusion
that shouts and show are not the way,
that noise and overstatement
will only serve to violate and dismay.

For when it is done,
how is the winning counted?

In
possessions and self-interest,
in
force and aggression,
in
offence or insults?

Or should it be in a respect,

for
courtesy and tolerance,
for
integrity and truth,
for
trust and friendship?

I have arrived at a conclusion.

IAN SOUTER

85

The Power of Love

It can alter things:
The stormy scowl can become
Suddenly a smile.

The knuckly bunched fist
May open like a flower,
Tender a caress.

Beneath its bright warmth
Black ice of suspicion melts;
Danger is dazzled.

A plain and dull face
Astounds with its radiance
And sudden beauty.

Ordinary things –
Teacups, spoons and sugar-lumps —
Become magical.

The locked door opens;
Inside are leaves and moonlight;
You are welcomed in.

Its delicate strength
Can lift the heaviest heart
And snap hostile steel.

It gives eloquence
To the dumb tongue, makes plain speech
Blaze like poetry.

VERNON SCANNELL

What's the Truth?

Last week
They said I ought
To turn the other cheek.
This week
After I turned – and ran
They said
That I should learn
To stand and fight;
To be a man.
That sounds to me
More eye for eye
And tooth for tooth.
But what's the truth?
Are they just fools?
Or is there sense in changing rules?

JOHN KITCHING

Why We Must Be Heroes

'Got no guts! that's their trouble,
Do you know, when I was their age,
I'd killed twenty men stone dead.
Got no respect! that's their trouble,
Do you know, when I was their age,
You could be shot for not saluting the King's picture.
Got no loyalty! that's their trouble,
Always questioning our morals and ethics,
That's the trouble today,
Young people don't want to die for their country.'

C. LIVESEY

Falklands Duty

'In the course of their duty,'
intoned the spokesman of the M.O.D.,
'2 ships have been sunk.
672 men are missing.'

'In the course of their duty,'
intoned the spokesman of the M.O.D.,
'a bomb landed on soldiers' barracks
killing 24 men.'

'In the course of their duty,'
intoned the spokesman of the M.O.D.,
'6 aircraft have been shot down
with the loss of 12 crew.'

'In the course of their duty,'
intoned the spokesman of the M.O.D.,
'leaders have agreed
to Strategic Arms Limitation Talks.'

'In the course of their duty,'
intoned the spokesman of the M.O.D.,
'soldiers are to dismantle
all nuclear weapons.'

'In the course of their duty,'
intoned the spokesman of the M.O.D.,
'the generals have made
100,000 soldiers redundant.'

'In the course of their duty,'
intoned the spokesman of the M.O.D.,
'the Cabinet is disbanding
this Ministry.'

'And finally,'
intoned the spokesman now redundant,
'does anybody need
a spokesman?'

LAURELLE ROND

Throw It Away

'What's this?' he asks.

'Don't know,' she replies.
'Looks old.
It's metal
And cold.'

'What's the pointed part?
And this curved bit?'

'I think it's a . . .
Killing machine.
Throw it away,' she says.
'It's not needed now.'

JONATHAN HART (14)

Bridge in the Sky

In the war you bombed our city without mercy,
And we lived as best we could amongst the ruins,
Now your warplanes drone again above our houses,
They are bringing food to our blockaded city,
But special planes flew low on Easter Sunday,
And it rained chocolate here in West Berlin.

THERESA HEINE

NOTE: *The Berlin Blockade happened between 1948 and 1949, and lasted a year. Food and coal were landed at the airfield the United States Air Force had built, and was distributed from there. A group of American pilots decided to do something for the city's children at Easter. They got a consignment of chocolate and flew low over the area around the airfield, dropping chocolate 'bombs' to the delight of the Berlin children.*

For the Christening of Princess Elizabeth, Later to be Queen Elizabeth the First

She shall be loved and feared; her own shall bless her;
Her foes shake like a field of beaten corn,
And hang their heads with sorrow; good grows with her.
In her days every man shall eat in safety
Under his own vine what he plants; and sing
The merry songs of peace to all his neighbours.
God shall be truly known; and those about her
From her shall read the perfect ways of honour,
And by those claim their greatness, not by blood.

WILLIAM SHAKESPEARE

Peace in a Bottle

What if peace came in a bottle,
and you drank it down
when the need arose?
'Here, take some of this,' the doctor might say.
Two spoonfuls when you're feeling cross
or when someone gets up your nose,
when you're sad or unhappy
or when you're about to hit the roof!
Two spoonfuls of this should stressproof you.

There could even be special kinds of drink:
'Diet-Peace' for those weighed down too far,
peace with an extra *ZING*, for the sportsman
seeking new performance peaks.

Each bottle is guaranteed to release
some sense of tranquillity within minutes.
So first decide what peace is to you:
an empty beach, a field after rain,
a sunset glow, a dreamless sleep.
Find somewhere comfortable to sit
then grip the cap and twist it round.
Let the feelings inside escape.

Then drink down deep on whatever's released
till you find yourself at peace with peace.

BRIAN MOSES

A Patch of Peace

Open eyes, in the dark,
are dazzled by starlight.

Open ears, by the sea,
hear unwritable songs.

Open hands, ungrasping,
receive uncountable riches;

an open mouth, and nose,
tastes, and smells, the rain.

Open the castle gate
to walk out, braver,

into a field of battles
where a patch of peace can work.

JANE WHITTLE

Keeping the Peace

Tiptoe gently, stepping on shells,
Building bridges, treading with care.
Fire new heavens, quench old hells.

Tunnel through mountains, fly over fells,
Carrying hope for all to share.
Tiptoe gently, stepping on shells.

Draw fresh waters from deep wells,
Drink new wisdoms, rich and rare.
Fire new heavens, quench old hells.

Speak the message the smoke ring tells,
Smoke from peace-pipes whispering prayer.
Tiptoe gently, stepping on shells.

Climb the steeples, ring the bells,
Make the new world stand still and stare.
Fire new heavens, quench old hells.

Sing your song in villanelles,
Peace will rhyme when war won't dare.
Tiptoe gently, stepping on shells,
Fire new heavens, quench old hells.

CELIA WARREN

On the Seventh Day

And on the seventh day
God rested
And He spake unto His creation
saying:

Thou shalt not
seize
squeeze
or otherwise
tease.

Thou shalt not
sneeze
wheeze
or exhibit other
noisy symptoms
of disease.

There shall be
neither creaking knees,
nor jangling keys.

Nor rough seas,
nor falling trees.

Nor honking geese
nor maddening fleas.

Definitely no buzzing
of bees.

And watch it,
you wallabies.

Let there be no crises,
nay, not so much as a breeze.

So cut it out. Knock it off! . . . PLEASE!

Thank you. At last.

PeaZZZZZZZZZZZZZZZZZZ.

IAN WHYBROW

To Every Thing

To every thing there is a season,
    and a time to every purpose under the heaven:
a time to be born,
    and a time to die;
a time to plant,
    and a time to pluck up that which is planted;
a time to kill,
    and a time to heal;
a time to break down,
    and a time to build up;
a time to weep,
    and a time to laugh;
a time to mourn,
    and a time to dance;
a time to cast away stones,
    and a time to gather stones together;
a time to embrace,
    and a time to refrain from embracing;

a time to get,
　and a time to lose;
a time to keep,
　and a time to cast away;
a time to rend,
　and a time to sew;
a time to keep silence,
　and a time to speak;
a time to love,
　and a time to hate;
a time of war,
　and a time of peace.

ECCLESIASTES III, i – viii

Index of Poets

JOHN AGARD   *The Soldiers Came*   47

JOAN AIKEN   *Ash Talks to Bone*   48

MOIRA ANDREW   *All in the Mind*   13

    Peace in Our Time   17

W.H. AUDEN   *Epitaph for the Unknown Soldier*   69

LAURA BLYTH   *Truces*   73

ASHLEY BULLARD   *Peace*   75

LI CHIN   *She a Brother, He a Hand*   66

PIE CORBETT   *Outbreak of Peace, haiku*   16

ANTHONY DICKINSON   *Bang! Bang!*   30

ECCLESIASTES   *To Every Thing*   98

ROSIE FILBY   *The Soldier's Home Coming*   51

JOHN FOSTER   *I Dream of a Time*   79

EMLYN FREEMAN   *Deprivation*   24

LOLA GAMESTER   *Not a Piece of Cake*   79

DOUGLAS GIBBONS   *Light*   62

WILFRID WILSON GIBSON   *A Lament*   53

THOMAS HARDY   *Christmas: 1924*   69

JONATHAN HART   *Throw It Away*   90

TREVOR HARVEY   *Caged Bird*   82

THERESA HEINE   *The Red Cross*   68

    Christopher's Song   83

    Bridge in the Sky   91

ADRIAN HENRI   *Newsflash*   37

FRANK HORNE   *Kid Stuff*   84

LIBBY HOUSTON   *Post-war*   59

SUSIE JENKIN-PEARCE   *Family Photo, '45*   18

101

JEAN KENWARD   *The Homecoming*   52
                Refugee   65
SAMEERA KHAN   *The Question*   26
JOHN KITCHING   *What's the Truth?*   87
URSULA LAIRD   *A Day Off*   19
C. LIVESEY   *Why We Must Be Heroes*   88
CHRISTOPHER MANN   *Desert Storm*   31
                    Arnhem   60
TOM MASTERS   *Falklands Hero*   63
ROBIN MELLOR   *After the Party*   36
ADAM MOON   *Russian Roulette*   41
BRIAN MOSES   *Don't You Know There's a War On?*   29
                Peace in a Bottle   93
JUDITH NICHOLLS   *Remembrance Day – 11th November*   54
JAMIE PARKINS   *The Search*   72
JAMES PARSONS   *Attacking Missile Base Three*   38
PAUL   *Why Must We Fight?*   25
WILLIAM PAYNE   *If Peace Went on for Ever*   74
JANIS PRIESTLEY   *Jimmy, Jimmy*   15
                   Bombshell   45
KATIE REDMAN   *Destroyer Destroyed*   25
LIAM RING   *Sunrise in Kuwait*   66
TONY ROBERTS   *Would You Swap?*   76
                Silver Dream   80
LAURELLE ROND   *Falklands Duty*   88
ANITA MARIE SACKETT   *School Bus Journey - Malta, 1946*   46
SIEGFRIED SASSOON   *Everyone Sang*   45
VERNON SCANNELL   *The Power of Love*   86
WILLIAM SHAKESPEARE
   For the Christening of Princess Elizabeth   92

AMY SHEARING   *Tiananmen Square*   64

POLLY SINCLAIR   *N.U.P. Report*   40

POLLY SMITH   *Peace*   16

IAN SOUTER   *My Heart Beats*   20

   The Conclusion   85

ROBERT SPARROW   *Encounter*   22

JAMES STEVENS   *Haiku Friendship Poem*   18

GEOFFREY SUMMERFIELD   *Waterloo*   34

CHARLES THOMSON   *Computer Game*   32

MEG GRANT TURNEY   *My Brother Coming Home*   50

JAMES WAIGHT   from *Harold*   48

CELIA WARREN   *Keeping the Peace*   95

RACHEL WELLMAN   *The Dove*   14

JANE WHITTLE   *A Patch of Peace*   94

IAN WHYBROW   *On the Seventh Day*   96

ELIZABETH WILKES   *Burn Your Lips*   23

JAMES WOLFE   *There Were No Potatoes*   70

Index of First Lines

After the party   36
An oil rig leaked a week ago   75
And on the seventh day   96
April 5th 1990   68

Bright,   66
Britons and Romans, Saxons and then Danes,   48
Burn your lips with scalding coffee;   23

Cable News Network bring you live and
  exclusive coverage,   31

Everyone suddenly burst out singing;   45

Flower   16
From our Laboratory comes -   76

'Got no guts! that's their trouble,   88

'Here,' said Mam. 'Hold one end of this old sheet   50
His hands rummaged   62
His was   80

I am peace   14
I don't want   19
I dream of a time   79
I found this small white church in Brittany   22
I have arrived at a conclusion   85
I ran across the long playground.   38
I saw a man on telly,   63
If peace went on for ever it would be dull and boring,   74
In 1943   59

'In the course of their duty,'   88
In the ocean a ship lies   25
In the war you bombed our city without mercy,   91
It can alter things: 86
It was cold and foggy,   83
It's good, coming home,   52

Jimmy, Jimmy?   15

Last night   45
Last week   87

My father.   51
My mother didn't know there was a war on!   29
My mum declares peace.   16
My spirits tighten   20

Napoleon, the roly-poly 'un,   34

One Saturday morning   73
Open eyes, in the dark,   94

PEACE!   17
Peace, for me, is a black and white photo,   18
Peace is a bird,   13
'Peace upon earth!' was said. We sing it,   69
Poppies? Oh, miss,   54

Red rose-buds stood there proud and tall,   64
Reports are just coming in that . . .   37

She shall be loved and feared; her own shall bless her;   92
skywards,   82

The ghost of a cuckoo   48
The National Union   40

The soldiers came   47
The wise guys   84
There were no potatoes.   70
They sat opposite;   41
They were part of the landscape,   46
This is a poem about peace,   79
This was my home.   65
Tiptoe gently, stepping on shells,   95
To every thing there is a season,   98
To save your world, you asked this man to die: 69
23.9.84   60
Two boys by firelight,   18

We who are left, how shall we look again   53
WHAM! WHAM! Zappa zappa!   32
What!   24
What do they know of war,   30
What do you   26
What if peace came in a bottle,   93
'What's this?' he asks.   90
When at last the gun shots cease   66
Why must we have war?   25
With bright blonde hair   72

Acknowledgements

All in the Mind and *Peace in Our Time* by Moira Andrew, reprinted by permission of the author.

The Dove by Rachel Wellman, *Peace* by Polly Smith, *The Question* by Sameera Khan, *Tiananmen Square* by Amy Shearing, *She a Brother, He a Hand* by Li Chin and *Not a Piece of Cake* by Lola Gamester, reprinted by permission of the authors, all of James Allen's Girls' School.

Jimmy, Jimmy and *Bombshell* by Janis Priestley, reprinted by permission of the author.

Outbreak of Peace, haiku by Pie Corbett, reprinted by permission of the author.

Family Photo, '45 by Susie Jenkin Pearce, reprinted by permission of the author.

Haiku Friendship Poem by James Stevens from *Letter to a Friend* (Penguin), reprinted by permission of the author.

My Heart Beats and *The Conclusion* by Ian Souter, reprinted by permission of the author.

Encounter by Robert Sparrow, reprinted by permission of the author.

Burn Your Lips by Elizabeth Wilkes, *Deprivation* by Emlyn Freeman, *Destroyer Destroyed* by Katie Redman, *Bang! Bang!* by Anthony Dickinson, *Light* by Douglas Gibbons, *Sunrise in Kuwait* by Liam Ring, *The Search* by Jamie Parkins, *Would You Swap?* and *Silver Dream* by Tony Roberts and *Throw It*

Everyone Sang by Siegfried Sassoon, reprinted by permission of George Sassoon.

School Bus Journey - Malta, 1946 by Anita Marie Sackett, reprinted by permission of the author.

By kind permission of John Agard c/o Caroline Sheldon Literary Agency *The Soldiers Came* from *Laughter is an Egg* published by Penguin 1990.

Ash Talks to Bone by Joan Aiken, reprinted by permission of the author.

My Brother Coming Home by Meg Grant Turney, reprinted by permission of the author.

The Soldier's Home Coming by Rosie Filby, reprinted by permission of the author, of Halesworth Middle School.

The Homecoming and *Refugee* by Jean Kenward, reprinted by permission of the author.

A Lament by Wilfrid Wilson Gibson from *Macmillan Collected Poems 1905-25*, reprinted by permission of Macmillan.

Remembrance Day from *Dragonsfire* by Judith Nicholls (Faber and Faber Ltd), reprinted by permission of Faber and Faber Ltd.

Post-war by Libby Houston from *A Stained Glass Raree Show* (Allison & Busby 1967), reprinted by permission of the author.

The Red Cross, *Christopher's Song* and *Bridge in the Sky* by Theresa Heine, reprinted by permission of the author.

ACKNOWLEDGEMENTS

Every effort has been made to trace the copyright holders of:

A Day Off by Ursula Laird

from *Harold* by James Waight

Kid Stuff by Frank Horne

Why We Must Be Heroes by C. Livesey

The Publishers apologise if any inadvertent omission or error has been made.

A Selected List of Fiction from Mammoth

While every effort is made to keep prices low, it is sometimes necessary to increase prices at short notice. Mandarin Paperbacks reserves the right to show new retail prices on covers which may differ from those previously advertised in the text or elsewhere.

The prices shown below were correct at the time of going to press.

☐	7497 0978 2	**Trial of Anna Cotman**	Vivien Alcock	£2.50
☐	7497 0712 7	**Under the Enchanter**	Nina Beachcroft	£2.50
☐	7497 0106 4	**Rescuing Gloria**	Gillian Cross	£2.50
☐	7497 0035 1	**The Animals of Farthing Wood**	Colin Dann	£3.50
☐	7497 0613 9	**The Cuckoo Plant**	Adam Ford	£3.50
☐	7497 0443 8	**Fast From the Gate**	Michael Hardcastle	£1.99
☐	7497 0136 6	**I Am David**	Anne Holm	£2.99
☐	7497 0295 8	**First Term**	Mary Hooper	£2.99
☐	7497 0033 5	**Lives of Christopher Chant**	Diana Wynne Jones	£2.99
☐	7497 0601 5	**The Revenge of Samuel Stokes**	Penelope Lively	£2.99
☐	7497 0344 X	**The Haunting**	Margaret Mahy	£2.99
☐	7497 0537 X	**Why The Whales Came**	Michael Morpurgo	£2.99
☐	7497 0831 X	**The Snow Spider**	Jenny Nimmo	£2.99
☐	7497 0992 8	**My Friend Flicka**	Mary O'Hara	£2.99
☐	7497 0525 6	**The Message**	Judith O'Neill	£2.99
☐	7497 0410 1	**Space Demons**	Gillian Rubinstein	£2.50
☐	7497 0151 X	**The Flawed Glass**	Ian Strachan	£2.99

All these books are available at your bookshop or newsagent, or can be ordered direct from the publisher. Just tick the titles you want and fill in the form below.

Mandarin Paperbacks, Cash Sales Department, PO Box 11, Falmouth, Cornwall TR10 9EN.

Please send cheque or postal order, no currency, for purchase price quoted and allow the following for postage and packing:

UK including BFPO   £1.00 for the first book, 50p for the second and 30p for each additional book ordered to a maximum charge of £3.00.

Overseas including Eire   £2 for the first book, £1.00 for the second and 50p for each additional book thereafter.

NAME (Block letters) ....

ADDRESS ....

....

☐ I enclose my remittance for ....

☐ I wish to pay by Access/Visa Card Number   ☐☐☐☐☐☐☐☐☐☐☐☐☐☐☐☐

Expiry Date   ☐☐☐☐